OTHER GODS

other gods

Regina O'Melveny

SOUTHWORD*editions*

First published in 2019
by Southword Editions
The Munster Literature Centre
Frank O'Connor House, 84 Douglas Street
Cork, Ireland

Set in Adobe Caslon 11.5pt

ISBN 978-1-905002-62-7

Contents

Acknowledgements

I am grateful to the editors of the following periodicals and anthologies in which some of these poems first appeared:

College English: "Swarms"
Conflux Press: "Fireflies"
Whiskey Island: "Formic Acid" and "Orb-Weaver"
Writing for Our Lives: "Fire in L.A."
The San Diego Poetry Annual: "Swallowtails"
Dark Matter: Women Witnessing: "*Corydalidae cornutus*"

"Tassajara" appeared in the anthology *The Garden*, edited by Jacqueline Bachar.

"Moth" appeared in the anthology *Beyond the Lyric Moment*, edited by Jim Natal, Cathie Sandstrom and Lynne Thomson.

for Bill

The Scent

Every morning the sun strings
black and gold beads
beyond my north window.
Bees rise to scent, then descend
to the hive, an earthenware
dome beneath the mock orange.

They bored a way into the hollow
sculpture three years ago though
I haven't called the beekeeper yet.
She warned me before when
they hived in the crawl space
under the house, then the fuse box –

you can't tell killer from ordinary
unless they attack. You have to
destroy them. But still I neglect to call her.
I'm fond of their constancy. Stir at dawn,
zoom to the flowers or resinous trees,
then all rejoin the hive at night.

Early one morning I stood
empty-headed too near the hive,
staring up at a hawk in the tree.
Two or three bees pelted
my cheek, but didn't sting,
simply rapped a warning.

Once at night under a sickle moon
after chucking rinds from a pail
to the compost, I put my hand on
the quiet clay hive and found it
humming within, deep string
endlessly plucked in the dark.

A friend sent me a postcard
from Crete, an ancient bronze seal –

two bees clasping a drop
of honey between them.
Three-thousand-year-old hives
were found in the Middle East.

Last month a lush swarm hung
like a scarf of small golden coins
from a green limb in my garden,
rare ornament a Minoan queen
might have draped
across her fragrant breast.

Or perhaps an offering
a steadfast friend might have arranged
on the queen's cold body after
an unexpected death. As I would've done
for my friend who died last month.

Adorned her with pendant bees
to sweeten her passage.
Yet within a few days
she was bone char and ash.
We assume that our friends
will walk alongside us forever.

But solace is not found in words
of comfort. We must live for every drop.
The heart may be a hive after all, hidden,
honeycombed and humming.
The soul, a sting, or sticky garment of light
or dusky bee escaping the lips

weighing no more than a single
mock orange bud.
The mind may be a brief scent
in a faraway field beyond the city, calling us
to glean wild nectar, so that
we might taste both worlds.

Moth

Though I search tirelessly
through insect handbooks, I can't find it
– the moth that flared midday – a lit coal
on the path to the summit.
I think of fire-handlers, -walkers and
-swallowers. Fire-starters.
I cupped it in my hands to show
my companions the red smolder
of front wings that leapt to
yellow on hind wings.
When I opened my hands
the moth didn't fumble away
but remained fanning its small flame
from the plump ochre wick
of its powdery body, tip-tapping its legs
across the grooved fate in my palm.
What salt text did it divine? Here is
a lifeline by fits and starts, a woman who
sleeps with mountains, with bees,
holy musters of sweet fuck and nectar.
Five fire ants will make all the difference
and then she'll flee her burning house
by means of orange spurts of kindling
under a Heraclitean sun. What salt text
did it divine? The whole world then
and its combustible nature.
The soul and its blood fuse.
The thousand hidden match tips of death's
conflagration, waiting in the dry punk
of the heart or bedded in the oily folds
of the brain, until the right nerve ignites.
And the moth? Spun by a gust it careened
into the twisted manzanita and fell,
snuffed by blue shadows.
All day I hoarded my wing-dusted hands
like a thief, determined not to lose
a single blistering grain of light.

Fireflies

I

Once I saw fireflies in a Mexican valley dark as ink,
my friend's voice flickers, a cool jar of light
thirty years after she rode the Mexicali–Ciudad de Mexico train.

The night sky mirrored their sparks with stars, above the train
that I also rode decades ago, my face pressed to the jostling window.
Stars enough to cast the train's shadow rushing

blackly beside us like water, knuckling over stones, scrub
and the glint of small creatures' eyes that watched us go by,
we who are spectral and inconsequential on this earth.

II

My sister once led me to a hedgerow studded with
pale green fireflies, the night I couldn't tell harsh words from
sorrowful holes punched in the black tin sky.

She called them *lucciole*, a word I spoke over and over,
lucciole, while children in an Umbrian chapel nearby
sang glories to a faraway God and his brown clay Son.

Yet there were other gods who didn't share our form
and tattooed their devotions, all sex and lumen
on the dense June air, while my sister and I could only weep.

III

Once I spent the night at the river's edge among fireflies
in darkness so deep I couldn't find myself. Couldn't even grope
the way. I knelt to the earthen floor, littered with crisp wings.

When everything stops, you can only scratch the dirt.
And when I touched a smooth round thing it was just
the knob of a bone, no door to the underground palace.

Though later, awaking in daylight, I briefly saw the outline
of hinges, a doorjamb fading in the ceiling of leaves above me.
Someday perhaps she will shine her green lanterns again.

Funnel Spider

She works
her spinnerets
in the coiled earth,
knits a mesh
that draws me down
through a lightless
tunnel of waiting.
A gauze, mute womb.
Limitless as the body's
red speech silenced,
as the children
I will no longer bear.

She asks me
to slough
little vanities,
errors gone dry.
In certain parts
of the world
a woman past child-bearing
strikes fields fallow,
unmans a lover,
turns wine to vinegar.
Better not cross
or ignore her.

The spider knows
where to set the lines.
Where to bend
the weave,
work the heft
of hunger.
In summer
the sage hills shimmer

with her dusty
shirred silk,
the pale
webbed mouths
of her prose.

This new
codex hums
in my body.
Words for tissues
of recollection,
lunar fluency,
small secretions of faith.
The way pulse is
weft to death's still warp,
and her deepest gift –
where to place
the empty center,
how to hold absolutely
nothing.

Tassajara

Last night near Suzuki Roshi's resting place
the yucca plumes blazed with moon.
A single bat feasted on
the invisible life of the air.

*

Spirit is also a pungent thing:
sage crushed underfoot,
feverfew brushed against the leg,
sweet bay laurel held to the nose,
skunk musk in the meadow,
musty oak humus, fresh coyote scat,
dry hot earth under my nails.

*

This morning bees swarm
to the dusky poppies
and leave the yellow dahlias
alone.

*

Emerald beetles
stud the shadow side
of the alder trunk.
How little we know
of these riches.

*

Touching my toe
to creekwater
I can't tell
exactly when it enters.
Likewise
I don't know exactly
when my heart opens.

*

This year swimming in the creek,
I taste the drought
ending.

Swallowtails

Two flare yellow and black,
tumble mid-air over the pond,
mating flap-scraps of summer.

Even as cumbersome caterpillars gorged
on ash leaves, they hold
fundamental sex and wings within.

Then the seclusion in dark quiet
pupae, mulling. Body tissues and organs
break down, rearrange for wings.

Who knows how it happens? We nod
to genes. But that explains nothing.
What double helix unzips beauty?

The child you once were, now woman
or man, finds the beloved. Becomes
the beloved. We always were.

Somehow dazzled we lift to joy
on erratic (puzzle the predator) wings
flung toward we know not where.

The Hunger of the Cecropia

After the hot rain,
big drops splotch the stone steps
in the summer garden.
A caterpillar, green as a sprout
emerges, thumbs the sky.
She ripples fantastic
tubercles tipped
with yellow, blue and red.
The cecropia sways
great mouthparts designed
for ravening leafy flesh,
sucking elm, birch and ash.
Such immense fabulous appetite.
And after the splendid season of glut,
a dry cocoon and winter fast.

In spring when dogwood opens
white four-winged blooms,
the pupa nibbles her crisp shroud,
wriggles free into night,
and fans full six-inch wings,
dusky fields with pale lunules.
No longer concerned with food,
her vestigial mouthparts useless,
the moth is voracious for a mate
and seeks his smell.
Later she lays her glistening eggs
and dies soon after,
her wings worn transparent
as she becomes the lambent
window she beats.

Hive

Bees refine a sweet fateful math,
all sixes, no sevens, they'll hex
your dress for a drop of honey.
Spill a malted and they're all over you,
bees that once frequented skep tombs in Malta.
Curl up little baby and sleep, larval.

The soul escapes with a radiant sting.
If you let the bee be,
the bee will let you.
But I worry about the teeming hive
they've wattled with comb in
my backyard sculpture.

Maybe the dome evoked a Malta
pinpoint in apian recall,
those parabolic tombs for the dead
who were buried in honey,
sticky bones the cross-staves of hive.
Still I'm not ready to die.

They may be killer bees. The queens
look the same. But whip-start
the blower and soon find out –
killer bees hate the drone of rivals.
African cuckoos started it all, guiding tribes
to hives thousands of years ago.

Bees learned that humans
would break up their fine geometry
while cuckoos got the remainders.
Soon bee-rage hooked to a gene. Later
keepers bred European with African
for a stronger strain but reaped irate.

Yet my honeys buzz tamely so far,
though when I walk by, my body smarts

with fear. Ssh, I tell my flesh, sh! Who knows
how loud the thin sweat-hum of panic is.
Still I want to taste what they know of
sun, scent and tongue-lapping flowers.

Which brings me back to six and sex,
how does one sex a bee?
It turns out they're all infertile females
(ovipositors gone to stingers)
except for a few larger lusty males that
ascend with the pheromone-laden queen.

And when it's all over, the males
jettison genitalia inside
the sovereign lady and die.
All for the good of hymenoptera's
well-ordered progeny.
But I've almost forgotten the pollen.

Those tibial baskets of lumpen gold
make or break the royalty.
When workers return to the hive
they shake their abdomens,
give up distance and plain directions
on how to get to the golden source.

Some life, eh? And sweetly precise.
If ancient Maltese could construct
human hives in honor of bees, then
by the same impulse I offer you home
dear tribe Apini, and promise
no poisonous smoke will drive you away.

Let waxen cells plump with eggs
and larvae, pupae prosper, let
honey and royal jelly increase, let my words
multiply to your renown, O queen
as you lap from your honeypot, plopping eggs
in the half-lit sixfold rooms of the world.

Orb-Weaver

Outside my fog-dampened window
the spider sets the spokes of her wheel,
turns the axis of my attention
as I scan a screen of light.

She draws silk outward, a guy line,
a thought to fasten on jacaranda leaves.
Her work, invisible like mine, tenders
a resonant thread from the deep of her belly.

She writes the philosophy of hunger mid-air,
elegant, practical and sacred.
She is my valve between worlds,
my mentor of manifold vision.

The spider tugs each line to test it.
I am pulled in, want to see
the whole thing, beginning to end.
She spirals from outside in,

tapping spinnerets to each spoke
as she passes, attaching the strand.
Spiders' silk tests stronger than cabled steel,
according to research in bulletproof vests.

What better way to halt the trajectory
of despair than this sticky net?
Orb-weavers each leave a mark
uniquely their own in the web.

I watch for the singular flaw that is hers
as I pivot around the ceaseless want
that lives at the center of things.

Corydalidae cornutus

otherwise known as the Dobsonfly,
flew to our failing lamp before
the hunchback moon could draw him away.

His crisp cellophane wings crossed
as he staggered up and down the table
snookered by sputtering candlelight.

A formidable drunk, three inches long
with segmented antennae and wangly
mandibles half the length of his body.

Predaceous, but not upon us,
the ancient creature clamped other
insects that bumbled into the lamp

while we sipped wine and plucked apart
the fried trout hooked that morning
when silvery fish blundered toward woozy sun.

One must always treat the god
in disguise as a guest at one's table.
So we let him stay though skanky.

Later I read that he is the most
primitive of all insects
that lumbers through metamorphosis.

Even the gods shift around
enacting their monstrous hungers.
Even now they maul our days.

Thanks be to rapacity then, to end of
summer and fish, to all the clumsy appetites
we can't untangle from our prayers.

Swarms

The first swarm hung
like iron shavings
from my horseshoe magnet
when I was ten.
Moiled on the branch
of an ancient oak
in the Cuyamaca mountains.
My father beside me, pointed
with his burled walking stick,
compared the buzz to
WWII bombers.

Twenty years later
a swarm agitated under
the eaves of my mother's
Umbrian house as she slept off
spent rage at my sister and me
in the hot afternoon.
While the two of us, also groggy
with anger, slumped in the red
metal garden chairs.
Painted bees dried
on her recent self-portrait.

Three more years passed
before the next swarm
in a friend's summer garden,
congealed fist of sex
on the lemon tree,
queen at the center
encrusted with drones,
workers attendant to hiving lust
as we considered what lay couched
in the long afternoons
of our marriages.

Now nine years later
the bees' condensed flight
mimics subatomics,
cloud-chamber scribbles
that mark the fields
of the invisible.
My husband and I gather up
our picnic and watch
the bees clump, sensing that
the world as we know it
has ended again.

The Best Time to Plant

When the first monarch flashes
across my yard this September,
advertises its singular orange
and black inedibility
conferred by milkweed,
my appetite for the unknown leaps
like a compass needle
within the butterfly's brain,
awakens the old urge south
where it's never been before,
this journey that takes
generations of monarchs to complete.
I change course and no one knows.
Gray whales will soon descend
from the Bering Sea, hugely pregnant.
White-crowned sparrows already
dapple the thicket of red honeysuckle.
Then rain. The ants move in,
nest in the Garland stove's back-burner.
This is the best time to plant
in my part of the country.
Leaves may not multiply with
the blatant redundance of summer
but all winter long the white roots
will spread and finger the way.

Formic Acid

Working late at my desk
I absently lift a hand to my neck,
something crawling there.
Inspect the smeared trail
on my thumb, a red desert ant
reeking of creosote bush.
A huge stench for an insect
the size of a vanishing point
which now approaches,
fills the end of the tunnel
I want to escape.
The light only
a contour of darkness.
The ant bears down
on the soft machinery
of my loneliness.
Freighted with the death
that's not quite done.
Mandibles on the detached head
still widen in threat
toward the tip of my pen.
I finish it off
but the rank odor goes on.
As a child I skipped along
a line of ants
just for something to do.
Watched them scurry
around their dying.
Horrified at what I had done.
How it could be done
so easily.
Three more ants jitter
across the desk
and fidget with the dead one.
The work is never finished.

Fire in L.A.

El Día de Los Muertos
The Day of the Dead

Tonight the mountains,
black cardboard cutouts,
glare fire and smoke.
The city curls back, grimaces
like the lit edge of a newspaper.

Trees, sagebrush, animals,
houses, sofas, books
and memory incinerate,
spreading a soot haze that
smudges the city.

We slowly learn the forms
of charred wood, melted
lawnchairs, single chimneys
and silverware magnified
at the bottom of pools.

Last year I watched the city
blaze against the verdict
given to police/assailants.
At first I too wanted
something to burn.

Wanted to wield my own
torched broom. Wanted fire to
purify us the way New Year
bonfires in Italy consume the old
things cast into the street.

Three years ago
a plume of butterflies streamed
from a coastal canyon on fire.
The slower monarchs
flickered in smoke,

their flame-colored wings
become flame,
while others spilled out to sea,
an orange river dividing
north and south.

In the paper I read
L.A. Ringed by Fire,
our lives crisp as insect wings,
dry as the exhalations
of Santa Ana winds.

I light a candle and pray for
small words with the fierce instinct
of orange butterflies
against ranges and
ranges of ash.

The Locust, the Bee and the Spider

Sometimes at night
my skull softens
like damp clay in Tunisia
lying in wait for the single locust
who'll generate the horde
sinking her long, pointed abdomen
into my brain
depositing eggs
cuneiform in the grey flesh.
My skull softens
like warm wax in the hive
where the bee squirms
in dark hexagonal cells
thick with honey and stiff white larvae.
The spider knits
in the flesh of my palm
nesting her young between my fingers
making a womb of my hand.
I lie very still in my bed
generous as a corpse
giving myself to be made over.
When the sun rises
we'll all begin to hatch.

Forgotten

Sometimes I'm unaccountably urged to light, as when I clean out a closet
and all the stagnant grief accrued in things is flung away and freed.

I'm clearer, cleaner as if washed, sponged by a bristly grandmammá of all
the clay that caked my thoughts. My little deaths transparent.

I'm not even speaking of the final one yet but all the others,
the whole succession of sheddings that make up a life.

My friend Mary Ellen said, *You have at least twenty more years to shape*
your life.
She being seventy-two, twenty years older than me. *If I'm lucky,* I say.

Mary Ellen now gone, as I revise this poem. There is a harsh
reduction to learn in one's life. All those carnivorous years –

my family lineage of madness and disappearance. Is it possible
that now I'm weightless as a leaf doubled at the edge of the pond?

That's today; tomorrow may be a different poem, silted with qualms
and suffocating algae. Or stirred by a blunt dragonfly naiad

that lives underwater for years, scours the blurry pond for food,
then one day crawls out on a reed and sheds herself to find new faceted
eyes

and red-veined wings stiffly uncurling from her center. Though that's
nothing
compared to the crackling mid-air coupling with a swank mate,

then the quick eggs she'll drop in the pond, tiny descendants that fall into
fish mouths or whisking naiad mandibles or simply land plop in the
fertile muck.

Surely this is consolation. We'll all be forgotten, subsumed, all the fine
particulars, all the brouhaha. Consolation of consumption. Solace of mu

We're not as important as we thought we were.
What a relief among the infinite reeds that whisper hush, hush.

www.ingramcontent.com/pod-product-compliance
Lightning Source LLC
LaVergne TN
LVHW051023080826
845145LV00009B/2778

* 9 7 8 1 9 0 5 0 0 2 6 2 7 *